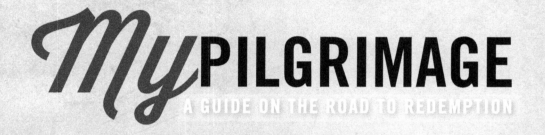

MYPILGRIMAGE

A GUIDE ON THE ROAD TO REDEMPTION

SETH TAYLOR

with DAVID GLENN TAYLOR

A **FLR** EXPERIENCE   **MYPILGRIMAGE**.com

Published in Kihei, HI by My Pilgrimage. Titles may be purchased in bulk for educational, business, fund-raising, or sales promotional use. For information, please e-mail: mypilgrimage3@gmail.com

Unless otherwise noted, Scriptures are taken from the Holy Bible, New International Version®,NIV®. Copyright © 1973, 1978, 1984, 2011 by Biblica, Inc.™ Used by permission of Zondervan. All rights reserved worldwide. www.zondervan.com.

Scriptures marked nkjv are from THE NEW KING JAMES VERSION. © 1982 by Thomas Nelson, Inc. Used by permission. All rights reserved.

The Library of Congress Cataloging-in-Publication Data is on file with the Library of Congress
ISBN: 978-1734997514

For all the pilgrims who yearn for the Road.

It stretches out before us and leads to redemption.

May we walk it with curiosity and courage.

And where we stumble, may our bruises be blessed.

Table of Contents

Welcome to the fallout
Welcome to resistance
The tension is here
Tension is here
Between who you are and who you could be
Between how it is and how it should be

Switchfoot, Dare You To Move

Welcome to the Pilgrimage...

This guidebook, just like the book **Feels Like Redemption: The Pilgrimage to Health and Healing** is about a paradigm shift. The chief aim of these works is removing the label of war and battle from our understanding of this issue of porn addiction and instead christening it as Pilgrimage: a Sacred Journey. I believe doing this will illuminate a path to true, long-lasting freedom.

First of all, I know addiction often feels like a war as opposed to something "sacred." That must be acknowledged, and I understand it as well as anyone who has walked this path. But we must also acknowledge that this might perhaps be because one of the most common characteristics of the human experience is that our perceptions become our realities. So, we feel this resistance inside of ourselves—like the Apostle Paul says in the New Testament: "I don't really understand myself, for I want to do what is right, but I don't do it. Instead, I do what I hate."[1] And then we are told this is a never-ending battle because of someone else's experience or reading of scripture or beliefs, and we believe it. The answer to this battle became suppression and oppression, mostly of our ability to feel and express desire. Rather than our bodies being understood as the Image of God, they're relegated to the level of corpses destined for burial.

This is the answer we often hear today: stop feeling (unless that feeling is guilt) and start controlling. You can't trust your emotions. We are told that God will heal us, but that we'll always struggle. Many even say that you simply will always be an addict.

---

1 *Romans 7:15 (NLT)*

Rather than seek out an understanding of what Jesus was talking about when he spoke of freedom and this mysterious thing he called "The Kingdom of God," we create a structured system of belief that keeps us contained and fenced in like so much cattle. And because of our need to hold to our religious beliefs, we label that fence "God" and pretend that life inside the corral is freedom. But perhaps you, like me, feel this is insufficient. Perhaps deep inside of you, in the places where you still feel and where your bodies and spirits still live free, you know there is something more. It is from this place where we begin to seek a new way of being.

And this is where your pilgrimage begins.

WHAT YOU ARE HOLDING IN YOUR HANDS IS UNIQUE.

This guidebook is designed to be your companion on a road that is narrow and difficult and radical and transformational and many other adjectives that I'll leave you to stumble upon. Like any road, it is your choice whether you walk it or not, but in order to discover what's over that next mountain, you have to walk, one step at a time. Think of this guidebook as a sort of reference you can toss in your backpack, sling under your arm, or set on the dash of your car on this journey. It will be a help to you both by giving you steps to take and then challenging you to actually take them.

Your time with this guidebook will be spent doing more writing than reading, more dreaming than thinking, and equal parts work and play. Of course, if you are seeking a deeper examination of this material, please read the book *Feels Like Redemption: The Pilgrimage to Health and Healing*. The materials in this guidebook are an extension of that source.

Jesus said: "Seek and you will find. Knock and the door will be opened to you." Meaning, the doors that have been opened are the ones you have knocked on. The real question is always and has always been, "What do you want?" This book is a sign pointing to a new way of seeing the doors that need to be knocked on. And this process (and guidebook) can be walked through again and again and again—and the results will always be new. That is the nature of the Spirit that lives within you.

This introduction chapter is a sort of "How To" for the rest of the book, so take some time to read each of the instructions and familiarize yourself with the process so that when you dive in, it is a seamless experience. It is not complex on a "doing" level and each chapter will have some similarities and some nuanced differences. For instance, after the teaching at the beginning of each chapter, you will have a "Body Check-In." Each chapter will have some leading questions that are meant to stir thought and push your experience down a progressive road. Each chapter will have journal space for you to deal with these questions.

Throughout the entire experience, feel free to doodle, draw, scribble, and make notes in any way that is helpful for you and anywhere in these pages. Sometimes, listening to some good music can be helpful when entering this introspective space. This book is your companion and this is your pilgrimage.

HOW TO DO THE BODY CHECK IN

(We'll provide the awesome sketch...)

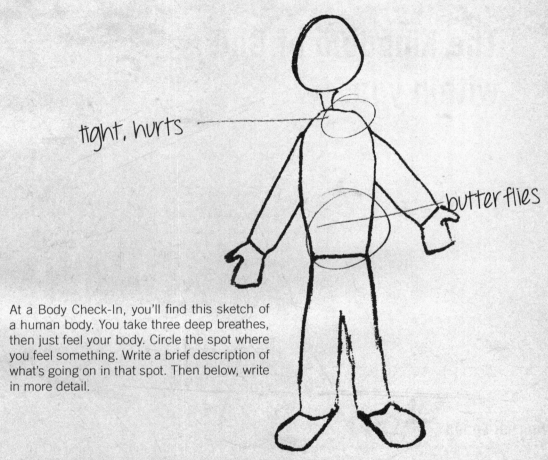

tight, hurts

butterflies

At a Body Check-In, you'll find this sketch of a human body. You take three deep breathes, then just feel your body. Circle the spot where you feel something. Write a brief description of what's going on in that spot. Then below, write in more detail.

Describe these feelings with as much detail as possible:

Example: My stomach has butterflies in it a lot of the time. In fact, I hadn't really noticed it til now, but I seem to have these butterflies most of my day. My chest feels a tightness also - it makes it hard to breathe, especially when I get stressed out.....

Write as much as you can.

The Kingdom of God is within you. *- Jesus*

We will often put quotes in these pages from people who have walked the road of pilgrimage. I dare you to memorize them.

If nothing else, you'll sound cool at dinner parties.

Journal Space

This is the space where we will ask questions designed to lead you along this path of transformation. The questions will most likely be spiritual/theological and therapeutic by nature. There are no "right or wrong" answers, but honesty and quiet reflection are necessary for this to be effective. Move slowly and breathe deeply while you do this. Don't rush this and try to get to the end of the book as quickly as you can. This isn't a race; this is your journey. The goal is that as this journey continues, your understanding of your path become more enlightened and you grow in awareness. So take your time — vulnerability is key.

Ex: What are some things from your childhood that have shaped the way you see God now?

My father was a pastor of a medium-sized church in North Dakota growing up. I suppose

the theology of our church had an impact on the way I see God. My dad was pretty strict.

I remember one time.....

Now you try answering the question:

Write as much as you want or need. There will be extra pages provided in the back for whatever you need or want to write about. If you fill up the space, flip to the journal space in the back, write a "continued from page…" and then keep going.

Another Leading Question will be presented:
This will be a continuation or "progression" from the last question. There will be several of these questions in each chapter. Depending on your level of engagement, this should allow you to map your transformation as it occurs.

Another Leading Question:
You get the idea.   Could make a heck of a memento some day.

Guided Meditation

Each chapter is going to finish with a type of meditation. Simply put, meditation is the practice of listening to God, while prayer is the practice of talking to God; one of our goals through this process is to help you learn how to "go inward" in a whole new way, because that is ultimately the process that will change you. Don't skip over the meditations thinking that the information is the only important thing here. Becoming "self-aware" can be helpful, but it will not change you. Your spirit must be awakened and that takes practice. Each meditation will have very specific instructions. Follow them as closely as you can.

Last Page of Chapter

In this space, there will be a final quote...

Read this quote over several times and allow it to wash over you. Sometimes, the quote will have a picture or an illustration. Whatever it is, it is meant to be meditated on.

- Seth Taylor

one more thing...

❧ Selah ❧

This phrase is sometimes translated from the Hebrew as something akin to *"pause and contemplate."* Meaning, at the end of each chapter, take some time to rest and reflect. Feel free to even repeat chapters if you feel the desire.

ok... let's do this...

CHAPTER 1

What are you medicating?

Noise, the grand dynamism, the audible expression of all that is exultant, ruthless, and virile—Noise which alone defends us from silly qualms, despairing scruples, and impossible desires. We will make the whole universe a noise in the end. We have already made great strides in this direction as regards the Earth. The melodies and silences of Heaven will be shouted down in the end.

- *The Demon Screwtape writing to his nephew Wormwood,*
  The Screwtape Letters, by C.S. Lewis

What Are You Medicating?

We must begin this paradigm shift by changing the questions we ask about both porn addiction and about ourselves. I want you to do something that might sound odd, but you are going to need to take a little vacation from feeling bad about your struggles with porn so you can fully turn your attentions to a more productive way of being. Understand that in this process, you are going to slip up. Heck, let's not even call it "slipping up"— let's just call it what it is: "medicating." You are medicating tremendous amounts of reppressed pain (or "energy")trapped in your body, and no amount of guilt or shame is going to transform you. So, if you can take a break from that, you'll do much better with this. And no matter what you think or feel about God being angry with you about this problem—please know that GOD IS NOT ANGRY WITH YOU. Not even a little bit. That feeling you have that convinces you God is ticked at you is called "shame" and it is a lie that lives inside you, the product of a gap in your consciousness and some other toxic stuff we'll get into later. For now, just understand that shame is a deep wound that exists inside of you—and as you learn to go inward spiritually (and emotionally—they are completely linked), you will discover the roots of that shame and wonder why you ever thought God was mad at you at all. (And that feels like freedom.)

So the only real question is, "What are we medicating?" Are you willing to go wherever that question may take you? Because the reality is that we are talking about cracking open a Pandora's Box of sorts. Everyone medicates—we use porn, or other substances, or religion, or work, or… pick your poison. Porn is unique because our sexuality is a mysterious and important function that keeps us connected to ourselves and to God and to the world, but we all medicate with something.

These are very deep, very real questions that must be asked. So, let us begin there. The next time you medicate, lay down the guilt about it long enough to ask the question about what you are medicating. I believe the medicine is close to the wound. Meaning, if we are medicating with porn, then that says something about the type of wound we are medicating. So before you go to your medicine and everything goes numb, try to feel the energy in your body that is demanding the medicine. Don't judge it as "bad" or "good" or anything else. Just try to feel it. Ask yourself (and the Holy Spirit) what it is. Understand? Awesome. Now, let's check in with your body.

BODY CHECK IN

Take three deep, slow breaths and sit completely still. Lay down if that feels more comfortable. The goal here is to feel what is in your body without thinking and judging—just observing. What do you feel in your body? Try to circle the part of your body where you feel something and then write about it in as much detail as you can in the spaces provided below.

Remember that feeling "nothing" is a definitive feeling. If you are numb, it is important to note that...

We are working under the theory that those uncomfortable feelings in your body, even if they're only numbness, are pockets of reppressed emotion, or reppressed energy, in your body. This repressed energy is what you are medicating. Anything can be medication. Porn and other addictive substances are obvious forms of this, but everyone varies in the medication their pain demands.

Some examples of medication include social media, sports, religion, and work. Sit for a while and try to think of what medications you use and why. Try to come up with your "Top 5" list, ranking your "drugs of choice" with no shame or guilt. Just be honest and reflect on it. Write a sentence or two about why that drug is ranked there.

Ex: I have a buddy who always told me that porn was #2 for him while chewing tobacco was #1. He didn't know why. But he felt that it was important for him to find out.

5

4

3

2

1

What situations dictate which medications you use? What effects do those medications have on those parts of your body you are learning to feel? Take your time and remember to breathe as you think and write about it:

We cannot selectively numb emotions. When we numb the painful emotions, we also numb the positive emotions.

- *Brené Brown,* *The Gifts of Imperfection: Let Go of Who You Think You're Supposed to Be and Embrace Who You Are*

The idea of reppressed emotion is rather simple and deeply complex at the same time. Essentially, as a child, you were designed to experience certain emotions in powerful and free-flowing ways. It is very much a part of the human experience for us to learn very early which emotions are safe to feel and which are not. Sometimes, we are virtually forced to stop feeling, such as in severely abusive home situations. But even in more healthy homes, we can still be taught to suppress to the point where it becomes almost as natural to the human experience as breathing.

Take some time to think about your childhood. You had a lot of feelings; some of them were safe to feel and some were not. The goal with this exercise is to reflect on your life and determine when and where your feelings were forced into the shadows.

In the following pages, reflect on your early life in this light. Yes, your parents must be a part of this experience. Whether they were intentionally hurtful in your life is one question, but even if they weren't, the fact remains—there are NO perfect parents. Resist the urge to defend your parents. Maybe you love them dearly, but they are still a part of this story. And we were all forced to suppress emotion. It is important we begin to find and speak the truth about what we needed to feel, because the truth is that some part of us is trying to heal those wounds. That's why you've started this pilgrimage. And your family life is an important stop on this road.

We know we're medicating. The question is: what pain are we medicating and where did that pain come from?

Let's begin some examination of your early life. If you had to guess, what pain are you medicating and where did that pain come from?

Guided Meditation

This will be a short meditation (5 minutes will do) with the goal of gaining the ability to observe yourself in your medication habit. As with most meditations, you will need a place that is quiet and solitary. Even your car will work. Feel free to set a timer for 5 minutes if you want to, but you can also do this for as long as you want.

We will begin every meditation with one minute of breathing and feeling the internal parts of yourself. The goal is to locate whatever reppressed emotion you are medicating.

Breathe as deep as you can and feel, don't think. (Knots in your stomach? Tight in your chest? Numb all over?)

When you feel like you have located some of this reppressed energy, use your imagination and see yourself in the process of heading to your medication. Whether that be pornography or TV or social media or some other thing—just watch yourself from a short distance.

Watch the process and try to observe the disconnection your other, imagined self is experiencing. Sit with that for a while.

Now take the following pages to write your observations of the experience. Can you feel compassion for your imagined self? What are your truthful feelings toward him or her?

Note: Sometimes this type of meditation can cause reactions in the body—as if the body is trying to kick the negative stuff out. If this happens (perhaps your body wants to cough, or scream, or cry…perhaps even vomit), just know this is ultimately a healthy thing. Try to allow your body to do what it wants to do. Your spirit is designed to heal you.

What was the experience like?

We shall not cease from exploration
And the end of all our exploring
Will be to arrive where we started
And know the place for the first time.

- T. S. Eliot

❧ Selah ❧

CHAPTER 2

Language

Words have no power to impress the mind without the exquisite horror of their reality.

- Edgar Allen Poe

Words, Words, Words

Language is a subtle yet important element to your suffering. The way you use language might be unknowingly protecting your unconscious pain; semantics is a major part of the human experience. So we're going to practice using language now. You may find it necessary to utter the words, "I am an addict" for the first time, or you might need to speak the truth about how you actually feel in your deepest depths. For example: if at your core, you experience abandonment, it can be damaging for a time to continue to hold on to the idea that "God is with you." Though it can theologically be said, "God is with you," we are talking about coming to a conscious peace with what you actually experience.

We are not speaking about theological truths in this chapter; we are speaking about your emotional truth, which is the kind of truth to hold to in this process of healing. If you feel alone, some wounded part of you is alone. And don't worry about hurting God. God can handle this. Defending God and our parents from our honest feelings is an unconscious way of fulfilling a role we believe at some level we have to play. It was given to us a very long time ago. Like it is our job to make sure God is okay or that our parents are okay instead of the other way around. This practice, called caretaking, is extremely common and is based in a deep emotional wound. For this healing experience to be valuable, we have to stop defending our parents and God and finally be where we actually are. So, in this chapter, we are going to make an attempt to write the words that more accurately describe where we really live internally. This will likely be difficult, so take a deep breath and gird your loins. But first, let's check in with the body.

BODY CHECK IN

Take three deep, slow breaths and sit completely still. Lay down if that feels more comfortable. The goal here is to feel what is in your body without thinking and judging—just observing. What do you feel in your body? Circle the part of your body where you feel something and then write about it in the spaces provided below.

Try to describe the feelings in your body in as much detail as you can (and remember that feeling "nothing" is a definitive feeling—if you are numb, it is important to note that):

The goal in this chapter is to work with words and whatever you feel in your body. Let's begin with some guided questions and journaling. It is important that while doing this exercise, you stay mindful of the experiences in your body that you just wrote about.

Question: How would you describe your struggles to a friend if you were telling them for the first time?

Journal as if you are speaking to that friend. Explain to your friend what you are doing about the issue(s). Imagine them with you if that is helpful.

Same question—different conversation partner. How would you describe those same struggles to your spouse/partner?

If you already have conversations about what you experience, write down the words and phrases you use to describe your struggles with that specific person. If you are single, think of a person you struggle to be vulnerable with—how would you describe this with them?

Every spoken word arouses our self-will.

- Johann Wolfgang von Goethe

Now go back over the last two journal questions/entries.

Circle words you use that are the same. Put a **box** around any words that changed because of the difference in conversation partner. Now write them in the journal space below.

Circled Words

_____

_____

_____

_____

_____

_____

Boxed Words

_____

_____

_____

_____

_____

_____

Circled Words Try to define each of these words in the way you used them.
Example: Lust - what I feel in the sinful part of myself that I can't control.

Boxed Words Why did you change the words? Did you realize you were changing them? Answer these questions for each of the boxed words.

Describe your struggles one last time.

This time, imagine that you are in a setting where you feel safe and at peace. It can be anywhere. Take two minutes to breathe and feel your body again before you do this. Then, when you are ready, journal about your struggles from a deeper and more brutal place. Yes, be brutal in your language. If you need to swear, have at it.

Catch yourself when you feel the need to defend God or your parents or anyone whom you might desire to protect from your feelings. Find new and more honest words to use. Be mindful of what you're feeling in your body (your body-experience).

Take the time to be honest. Your truth needs to come out.

Return to your body...

Check in with your body again. Take some time to go back to the body check-in page and make any additional notes needed there as to what you experienced after this journal exercise. Make a star next to the notes so you can compare before and after.

Accept everything about yourself – I mean everything, You are you and that is the beginning and the end – no apologies, no regrets.

- Clark Moustakas

A New Language

It is time for new words in your experience of God, yourself, and the world.

In the spaces below, write down new words that most accurately describe what you feel about your struggles. Use a thesaurus if you need to. Hold nothing back. Spare no one. Breathe while you do this and be mindful of what you experience in your body.

Guided Meditation

Now, go through the words you just wrote down and choose 4 or 5 that you can remember. These will be the words you will use as a prayer for this meditation. Like before, find a place to sit comfortably or lie down. If you get too sleepy when you lay down, that's okay—but perhaps sit up instead. Cover your eyes or close them—it is important that it is silent for this exercise, so if you have to go park your car somewhere, go for it.

Take one minute and breathe deeply and continuously.
Feel your internal body. Feel the re——ppressed emotion and try to locate it.

When you feel still enough, speak out loud the first word.
Direct the word to whomever needs to hear it, whether that is God, your parents, your partner, or yourself. Sit with the word until you are ready to speak the next one. Continue down the list and repeat it for as long as you need to. If any single word or phrase resonates emotionally, stay with it. An example might be, "I feel abandoned." You don't need to understand why you feel the way you feel. That will come in time. But it is time to speak the truth about what you feel.

Remember, it is very important to move energy out of your body if you feel the need to do so.
If you need to scream, grab a pillow or steering wheel or whatever you need and let it rip. The same goes for crying or puking or coughing. Just let your body and spirit lead you. Stay with this as long as you can and remember, if you feel nothing, that is feeling something. Feel the numbness without judging it or yourself.

Do this for a minimum of 10 minutes.
If it is difficult, that's okay. It's supposed to be. If it were easy, everyone would do it. Take these last few pages to write about what you experienced in the meditation.

The truth is rarely pure and never simple.

- Oscar Wilde, The Importance of Being Earnest

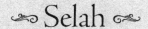 Selah

CHAPTER 3

What and why you believe

You never know how much you really believe anything until its truth or falsehood becomes a matter of life and death to you.

- *C.S. Lewis*

I am a relatively devoted sports fan.

Having been born and raised in Seattle, I naturally have endured a few things and very few of them have had anything to do with winning. We Seattleites have a few highlights we cherish, perhaps none greater than the 2013 NFL season when our Seahawks won our city's very first Super Bowl. But for the most part, we have spent a lot of energy over the years trying to pick ourselves off of the proverbial mat and gear up for one more try.

Maybe this is the year. Maybe this is the guy. Maybe…maybe…maybe

In 2010, my beloved Mariners kicked off their annual marketing campaign with the slogan "Believe Big." I remember thinking that was a poor choice. Before mid-season even rolled around, the M's were out of contention for any type of playoff race and the season was another "rebuilding year." It's tough to "Believe Big" when there is no reason to believe—those who do this are labeled "insane." It's not a normal function of humanity. The Mariners were bad and everyone knew it. And they had been bad for a very long time. Some of us had come to "Hope Big" and some even probably took risks and "Bet Big," but for any of us to "Believe Big," we needed to experience something new, some display of power that would take the hope we had and place it in the category of the real.

It seems to me that it is time for all of us who claim to be pursuers of the truth to come to grips with this simple fact: belief has no actual power beyond our own psychology. What we believe can make us take action, and that can be pretty powerful for good or bad, but believing in a God who can heal and *experiencing healing* are two vastly different things. [2]

Our stories have implications for each other. This is why Jesus described The Kingdom of God to be something like the wind. You might not see it, but you'll see the evidence of it. [3] Faith is having the courage to step into the unknown because of the evidence of the truth, whether the beliefs are the same or not. If your perspective is that your beliefs must match a creed or doctrine of some sort, then the best you can hope for is control masked in religious language as you seek affirmation from the people and environments you place around you.

So in this chapter, we are going to allow for the unknown. This will feel very much like a journal reflection. We are going to examine what we believe and why we believe it. The next chapter's exercise will take us further into questions surrounding belief, but for now, let's begin with a check-in with the body and then dive into some questions.

2 *An example of belief gone good: Mother Teresa said that she believed that Jesus was literally present in "the least of these". This infected her everyday presence with the poor. For an example of the bad, see 9/11.*
3 *Gospel of John, Chapter 3*

BODY CHECK IN

Take three deep, slow breaths and sit completely still. Lay down if that feels more comfortable. The goal here is to feel what is in your body without thinking and judging—just observing. What do you feel in your body? Circle the part of your body where you feel something and then write about it in the spaces provided below.

Try to describe the feelings in your body in as much detail as you can (and remember that feeling "nothing" is a definitive feeling—if you are numb, it is important to note that. Also, if you are doing these meditations, you might feel things changing a bit by now. Make sure to take some time and note any changes.):

Let's start with some simple lists.

Top 5 lists can be fun, but in this case, they may be difficult. Observe yourself as you do this. We're going to do a few of these. Honesty is paramount.

In the spaces below, list five things you believe about God. Try to limit each thing to one sentence or statement. Ex: "I believe God loves me," or "I don't believe God exists."

1. _____

2. _____

3. _____

4. _____

5. _____

Next, in the spaces below, list 5 things you believe about yourself. Anything is fair game. You will find it more helpful to keep it in the realm of traits as opposed to answers like, "I believe I really like ice cream," although if that is all that comes to mind, that will still be useful to work with.

1. _____

2. _____

3. _____

4. _____

5. _____

This time, go back to the first list and think about why you believe these things about God. Then in the spaces below, write down the why for each statement of belief. Try to trace each reason as far back as you can. Statements like "Because it's true," for instance, will have a deeper question behind them (e.g. "Why do you believe that's true?"). An answer like, "Because the Bible says so," will have a deeper question also: "Why do you believe the Bible is true?" Every question can be traced to a deeper place.

Take as much time as you need in order to break these beliefs down to their core. Make a special note of places where the *why* is of a supernatural nature. And know that "I don't know" is a more than acceptable answer.

1.

2.

3.

4.

5.

Now do the same with the list of beliefs about yourself.

1.

2.

3.

4.

5.

For the good that I want, I do not do, but I practice the very evil that I do not want. But if I am doing the very thing I do not want, I am no longer the one doing it, but sin which dwells in me.

- The Apostle Paul, The Book of Romans, Chapter 7

Why do we do what we do? What are the core motivations of human existence?

I recently watched one of my favorite movies, *The Pursuit of Happyness*, and was struck by the monologue Will Smith's character speaks regarding the Declaration of Independence. Smith's character, Chris Gardner, is struggling and he starts having a bit of a revelation. He says:

> **"It was right then that I started thinking about Thomas Jefferson and the Declaration of Independence and the part about our right to life, liberty, and the pursuit of happiness. And I remember thinking how did he know to put the pursuit part in there? That maybe happiness is something that we can only pursue and maybe we can actually never have it. No matter what. How did he know that?"**

Do you ever feel like you can relate to that? I believe all people everywhere are seeking happiness above all things. We do what we do because some part of us ultimately believes this is the thing that will make us happy, including our pursuit and worship of God. We are driven to experience abundant life. We were put on this earth to delight in the everyday. As children, we find that happiness in the safety and security of our parents. Very few of us experience this in a complete way. Then as adults, we unconsciously run as hard as we can to recover all the things that we lost so early on. That, I believe, is why we do what we do.

On the following pages are some questions to ask and answer of yourself. Remember there are different parts of you, but the things you do indicate what you believe you must do in order to acquire what you want. Also remember that "I don't know" is a perfectly acceptable answer. These questions are meant to create self-awareness, not judgment.

So, as you answer them, stay outside them as the observer. Feeling guilty or shameful will not help you, so give yourself a vacation from that and just notice things.

What do you want most for your life? (Try to pinpoint three things)

What are you doing to achieve these desires?

Looking at porn or medicating with a substance of any kind (even "socially acceptable ones" like sports or work) is an action of internal belief. Some part of you believes these actions will move you closer to the things you most want. How, if at all, are these actions helping you get what you want?

In light of all of this, what do you believe the word "choice" means? How does that apply to you? How do belief and choice work with each other? How do they work against each other?

Guided Meditation

The goal for this meditation is to observe the body. Read through everything you just wrote out loud. As you do this, breathe deeply.

Read slowly and patiently.

Be still inside and observe how reading these things makes you feel internally.

Make changes to the things you wrote if you want to.
But ask yourself each question again and continue to breathe deeply. Allow emotion to rise. Accept whatever comes.

Do you believe God is present with you in the middle of this?
Write down some thoughts on what you experienced as you read through your journal.

Others, I am not the first,
Have willed more mischief than they durst:
If in the breathless night I too
Shiver now, 'tis nothing new.

More than I, if truth were told,
Have stood and sweated hot and cold,
And through their veins in ice and fire
Fear contended with desire.

Agued once like me were they,
But I like them shall win my way
Lastly to the bed of mould
Where there's neither heat nor cold.

But from my grave across my brow
Plays no wind of healing now,
And fire and ice within me fight
Beneath the suffocating night.

- A.E. Housman, A Shropshire Lad

⤳ Selah ⤳

CHAPTER 4
The function of belief

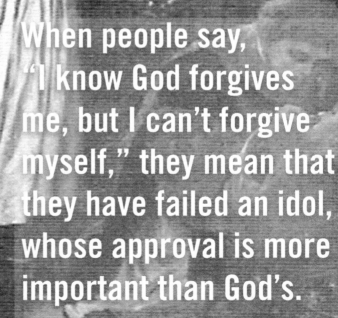

When people say, "I know God forgives me, but I can't forgive myself," they mean that they have failed an idol, whose approval is more important than God's.

- Timothy Keller,
Counterfeit Gods: The Empty Promises of Money, Sex, and Power, and the Only Hope that Matters

It's time to dive deeper.

Having spent some time thinking and writing about what we believe and why, let's ask the deepest question regarding belief: what role do our beliefs play in our lives? What is their function? For an illustration, have a close look at the painting opposite this page. This is a depiction of the rite of sanctuary being enacted by a priest of the church in the middle ages. For a few centuries in some parts of Europe, people could find sanctuary from arrest or attack within the walls of the church and under the wings of the priest. Such was the power of the church, and more importantly, the power of the belief systems of the day.

When you look at the painting, you can almost see the force of the cross holding back the armies of invaders. The priest stands in his authority, a representative of God himself. As you look at this picture, what is the force holding back the invaders? Is it magic? Is it the invisible hand of God? Is it some international law that must be respected?

Or is it belief? Is it an idea planted so deeply in the minds of the soldiers about the nature of God that they would not dare cross that line? What are they afraid of? Surely they aren't afraid of the priest hitting them with the cross? Are they afraid that if they cross that line and do what they want, they will go to hell? Take some time to study the picture and the faces of each character. How is belief asserting itself as another character in this depiction?

Of course, when we talk about the function of belief, we are naturally talking about the nature of idolatry. The idols of the ancient days were lifeless statues endowed with some type of magical quality because of the beliefs placed upon them. They were gods constructed in the image of man—and not just because man melted down some gold and shaped it into the image of a calf. The people of Israel were fed up with the mystery of God—they grew impatient and wanted something they could get their arms around. They wanted something that would "go before them." In other words, give me something I can see, touch, feel. Give me something that will fill the void I have at the deepest places inside of me. I need to experience something.

It's easy to understand porn and sex addiction in this way. The images we view serve the purpose of giving us something we can get our arms around. They protect us from having to feel the pain and anxiety that is locked inside of our bodies. But I believe the real crux of this is not necessarily that we have unconsciously created an idol out of sex and pornography, but rather that in our unconsciousness and pain, we create idols out of everything. We create gods everywhere. It's is a major characteristic of the human condition.

So, in this chapter, we are going to continue the work you did in the last chapter: the deconstruction of your beliefs as the thing holding you together—and the awakening of your spirit and discovery of the truth of what you are experiencing internally: your emotional truth. As always, let's begin with a check-in in your body.

BODY CHECK IN

Take three deep, slow breaths and sit completely still. Lay down if that feels more comfortable. The goal here is to feel what is in your body without thinking and judging—just observing. What do you feel in your body? Try to circle the part of your body where you feel something and then write about it in the spaces provided below.

Try to describe the feelings in your body in as much detail as you can (and remember that feeling "nothing" is a definitive feeling—if you are numb, it is important to note that. Again, if you are doing these meditations, you probably feel things changing a bit by now. There is also probably more sensitivity to what you feel. Make sure to take some time and note these things.)

Allow your emotional truth to breathe free.

Diving right in, the goal here is to find out where your beliefs have failed you and allow your emotional truth to breathe free. This is not an easy process, but as they say, the *hard* is what makes it great. We aren't trying to take your beliefs away from you. You can believe whatever you want. We are simply trying to reveal the places where you have unconsciously asked your beliefs to do something they weren't meant to do— hold you together and keep you from feeling the pain you are medicating and thus keeping you in pain. Your emotional truth can be painful to experience, but it's also the place where freedom starts to shine over the horizon. Keep your attention on your body as you do this. If you are truly engaging these questions, you'll feel it.

Think about your life as if it is a movie you're watching. Below are listed the characters in the human story. These characters exist in your life and have each played a role in where you stand today, whether by their activity in your life or the lack thereof. Sit with each character—do some character analysis— and write something about the role they have played in your life as it pertains to your addictions or primary struggles. Ask yourself, "Have they helped me? Hurt me? Just stood back and watched me?"

God

Mom

Dad

Siblings

List other characters who were primary for you and what role they played.
(Ex: Coaches, pastors/youth pastors):

Take a few deep breaths and feel your body. If something during that exercise triggered you, observe it and feel it.

Now read back over what you wrote about each character. But read out loud and change it into a prayer spoken to each character. So if you said, "God has been there for me every step of the way," read it out loud as, "God, I've believed in you my whole life but you're not there! I feel alone." Imagine each character sitting there with you as you speak this to them.

It is very important that you feel your body as you do this. If you begin to speak belief systems that contradict your emotional truth, you will experience that in the body. (Ex: if you feel abandoned by your mother, telling her that you're grateful for doing her best will cause a stir within. Just allow whatever you feel to be acceptable. If you feel the need to let it out and even direct it towards that person, do so safely. If you need to scream, grab a pillow and let it go into the pillow. If you need to cry, try to let it flow.)

Afterward, journal a little bit about the experience.

Eloi! Eloi! Lama Sabacthani?!

- Jesus of Nazareth, as recorded in the Gospels, in Aramaic

He allowed himself to be swayed by his conviction that human beings are not born once and for all on the day their mothers give birth to them, but that life obliges them over and over again to give birth to themselves.

- Gabriel García Márquez, Love in the Time of Cholera

It is called *The Cry of Dereliction...*

...the exclamation made by Jesus on the Roman cross of crucifixion all of those years ago. I've heard it said that this was the moment that God lost everything. It's almost as if the life of Jesus was a process of becoming human and that there on the cross, Jesus fully merged with the experience that could be characterized as the most human of experiences— we feel disconnected and cut off from the source of life. That is the experience of crucifixion: the loss of all of the things we thought made us okay. This what so many of us experience internally and this is why we turn to porn and other substances and form belief systems that claim such concrete "rightness," whether we experience it or not. We are, in some existential way, hanging on crosses, staring at the sky for any sign of light.

Perhaps the most intense thing for us to lose is our identities. And when we start to loosen the grip our beliefs have over our lives, we find our identities start to shift. So much of our sense of who we are is falsely wrapped up in what we believe. So often times, we have to put to death our identities and the belief systems that surround them in order to experience the resurrection to follow.

Understand, I am not saying, "Stop believing what you believe." I am saying you must kill any need you have for your beliefs to be the absolute truth for everyone in the world. Embrace the phrase, "I don't know." Apply this to yourself, God, and the people around you. Begin to seek a new truth— not one you can believe in, but one you can experience. Take a deep breath.

Know that your beliefs are like sand slipping through your fingertips.

Take some time to think about this question before you answer.

Breathe deeply and feel your body as you contemplate this. In the following pages, write a few stories about when you experienced love. They can be from any time in your life—but try to remember the feeling.

When we talk about truth, there is what we believe and then there is what we experience.

That part of you that is in pain and seeking medication has experienced a great deal of hurt and cannot be freed by being told something to believe. It needs to experience something real; the stories you wrote earlier represent that experience. It is time to seek more experiences of that nature, both externally and internally.

In the following exercise, we will do both.

You don't think your way into a new kind of living. You live your way into a new kind of thinking.

- Richard Rohr

Guided Meditation

Below is a prayer written by Henri Nouwen in his book, *The Only Necessary Thing: Living a Prayerful Life*. I've split it into two parts.

Close your fists, palms up, and take three deep slow breaths. Then begin to read part one aloud. Speak it to God and reflect on it inside of yourself.

Even if you do not believe God is there, speak it into that void. Read it over and over.

Remember to breathe and feel your body. Do this for at least 10 minutes.

When you are ready, conclude by reading part 2 three times aloud. Don't rush yourself—breathe deeply until your mind is calm and you are as present as possible. Don't open your fists unless you feel like you should.

Dear God,

I am so afraid to open my clenched fists!
Who will I be when I have nothing left to hold on to?
Who will I be when I stand before you with empty hands?

Please help me to gradually open my hands
and to discover that I am not what I own,
but what you want to give me.

❧ Selah ❧

CHAPTER 5

Triggers

Man's task is to become conscious of the contents that press upward from the unconscious.

There is no coming to consciousness without pain.

- Carl Jung

The word trigger is a *tricky* one.

When I was a porn addict, a lot of what was being written about the issue employed that specific word in this way:

You are sitting in traffic and a van pulls in front of you with an ad that features of a beautiful woman in a skimpy bikini. This upsets you because you're working so hard to avoid all the triggers, but they always seem to find you. And in that moment, something happens in you—your addiction has been triggered. You feel a numbness start to set in that may have faint senses of queasiness or your heart starts beating real fast. Maybe you start to sweat a little. But in some way, you start to separate from yourself and are driven to take this experience to its inevitable conclusion.

In the book, *Feels Like Redemption: The Pilgrimage to Health and Healing*, my brother and I engage in a thorough critique of this way of thinking, but in this space, all I want to do is change the definition of the word trigger to something that is not only deeper, but also simply more helpful. In chapter 1 of this guidebook, we talked about medicating our reppressed pain. Triggering that reppressed pain is the only way we can find out where it is so that it can be healed.

The woman on the van isn't the trigger—she's the medication. Triggers are more likely the things that cause you stress: things like relationships (spouse, parents, kids, boss, pet, etc.), money issues (these are huge), or performance issues (sports, work, school). Where this old paradigm I mentioned would locate the problems you have outside of yourself—like the porn industry or that woman who wears her shorts a little too short—the paradigm I am talking about locates the problem within you. That crud in your stomach needs some pain-killer to stay numb and bedded down. As if it has a will of its own, your pain is invested in staying put in its home inside the body. It's been there for a long time and is not going to go quietly.

So, in this chapter, we are going to think, pray, meditate, and write about triggers. We are going to seek out those things that were placed in your life to show you what your pain is and where it is stored in your body. In a way, we've already been practicing this with the check-ins with the body, so let's continue there.

BODY CHECK IN

Take three deep, slow breaths and sit completely still. Lay down if that feels more comfortable. The goal here is to feel what is in your body without thinking or judging—just observing. What do you feel in your body? Try to circle the part of your body where you feel something and then write about it in the spaces provided below.

In the space provided, try to describe the feelings in your body in as much detail as you can (and remember that feeling "nothing" is a definitive feeling—if you are numb, it is important to note that.

Again, if you are doing these meditations, you probably feel things changing a bit by now. There is also probably more sensitivity to what you feel. Make sure to take some time and note these things.

NOTE—if you need help feeling the body, then like a movie in your mind, replay a scenario recently where you have been triggered. Perhaps an argument with a loved one or a stressful experience at work or with money.

Take some time to think.

Listen to some reflective music if you need to. Breathe for a while and feel your body. When you're ready, use the spaces below to list the 5 things that trigger you most, ranking them from least intense to most intense. Start with the #1 thing that triggers you. Write a short description of what it is about that thing/person/situation that triggers you and how. (Ex: For me, I would have written:" #1 with a bullet—my wife." And then I would have started listing all the ways and reflected on it a bit.) Be as detailed as you can.

In the spaces across from your descriptions are corresponding lines where you are going to try to remember and describe the experience in your body when you are triggered by these things. If you need to, close your eyes and take a few deep breaths and then recall the specific situations that trigger you—and then feel your body as you do this. Try to locate in your body the pain that is being triggered. Remember to be aware if you go numb. That's a very specific feeling and is very important.

1

TRIGGER

2
TRIGGER

3

TRIGGER

4
TRIGGER

5
TRIGGER

Each one of these triggers is a road map showing you the way to the pain that must be healed in your body in order to gain freedom and peace.

You won't always know what pain is being healed. For instance, the first thing that healed for me when I started asking these questions about what was going on inside of me was my porn addiction. I believe that was because my greatest prayer (and greatest intention) was to be healed of that specific issue. When that cleared, I was able to see my other issues more clearly and that is when I started going after the depression, anxiety, and poverty.

Now, read back over these journal pages you just wrote. Read slowly and reflectively. In the following pages, corresponding to the number, write in detail what you wish to see changed about each situation. Try to focus on your responses, both internal and external. As opposed to, "I want her to stop treating me this way," try to see yourself in the situation. Ex: "When she treats me this way, I want to be able to feel calm inside so that I can respond in a way that brings peace and clarity instead of escalating the situation." As you do this, it can be helpful to become "The Watcher" (the observing self)—see the situation in your imagination again and instead of being the person that is triggered, stand back and watch yourself being triggered. Observe it and ask yourself how you would rather be feeling and responding.

1

2

3

4

5

The cure for the pain is in the pain.

- *Rumi*

My grace is sufficient for you, for my power is made perfect in weakness.

- *The Word of God spoken to the Apostle Paul in 2 Corinthians, chapter 12*

Guided Meditation

In this meditation, we are going to do some simple visualization (or "guided imagery"). Go someplace quiet where you can sit or lie down in a stance that is relaxing and easy to concentrate. Close your eyes and begin breathing deeply—try to breathe for at least three minutes, focusing on filling your whole body with air. Feel your body as opposed to letting your mind race. Listen to your breath.

Now pick the most pressing of the triggers you just wrote about and recall the last time it happened. Taking the stance of "The Watcher" again, observe the experience. Take your time: there's no need to rush through this. As the trigger begins, when you are ready, allow the part of you that is watching the situation to step in and help the part of you that is being triggered. Whether that is through coaching or comforting, allow this part of yourself to be in charge. Do this as long as it takes. Recall as many situations as you want and act as "The Watcher" in each.

What you are doing in this type of meditation is allowing your spirit to rise up and bring wisdom and peace to the situation. It is a gift of God that each of us is given and that can be accessed anytime we choose. We only need to get ourselves out of its way.

When you have finished with this process, before you get up or go back to your life, breathe deeply three times and after each breath, say this prayer:

I am not my pain.
My pain is my teacher.

The things you have written in this chapter represent the door to freedom.

Your triggers are your teachers.

They are the signposts pointing to the pain you are medicating with your addictions and control mechanisms. You only need the courage to walk into them, knowing that the problem isn't you —but being aware that the problem is *inside* you.

Of course the people and situations that trigger you need to change, and they will in time. But you cannot change them. You can only change yourself.

Selah

CHAPTER 6

Authority

Illustration by Anastasia Ward

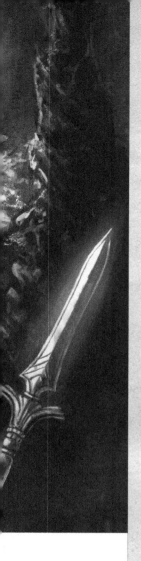

I feign that devils can, in a spiritual sense, eat one another; and us. Even in human life we have seen the passion to dominate, almost to digest, one's fellow; to make his whole intellectual and emotional life merely an extension of one's own—to hate one's hatreds and resent one's grievances and indulge one's egoism through him as well as through oneself. His own little store of passion must of course be suppressed to make room for ours. If he resists this suppression he is being selfish. On earth this desire is often called 'love.' In Hell I feign that they recognize it as hunger.

- CS Lewis, from the preface of The Screwtape Letters (1961)

Authority is the opposite of war.

If the USA had authority over Saddam Hussein, we would never have gone to war in Iraq. Our president would have simply said, "Hey—cut it out," and been answered with, "Yes, sir, Mr. President sir." And things would have changed.

Everywhere Jesus went, he spoke with authority and healed with authority and then taught his disciples to do the same. So my desire is that we not only seek an awakening of our spirits, but of the authority that comes with that. This is the thing that will allow us to change the world and ourselves. So, we must first learn to exercise this authority within our bodies. There is a very good chance that one of the reasons that you have struggled with addiction and the myriad of ailments that travel in addiction's wake is because you have no awareness of your authority. The darker stuff in your body only has the power you give it. That's one of the unique aspects of the energy of fear: it's an illusion that can absolutely cripple someone. But, at some level of consciousness, it's a choice.

So, in this chapter we are going to do a little probing around. This will not require you come to a new belief system, but it will require you to take yours and open them just enough to allow for the possibility of something new. There will be less thinking and more feeling in these exercises. And yes, if you are invested in this, you may experience something radical. So let's begin with the body check-in.

BODY CHECK IN

Like always, take three deep, slow breaths and sit completely still. Lay down if that feels more comfortable. The goal here is to feel what is in your body without thinking and judging—just observing. What do you feel in your body? Try to circle the part of your body where you feel something and then write about it in the spaces provided below.

On the following pages, try to describe the feelings in your body in as much detail as you can (and remember that feeling "nothing" is a definitive feeling—if you are numb, it is important to note that. And considering the subject matter of this chapter, you may begin to feel things that are "in you" but not "of you." If that is the case, make sure you make detailed notes of what it feels like.)

Let's begin with some questions for the head.

Remember there are no wrong answers here. We are working from a space of felt experience and consciousness, not belief—so you and I can disagree and still find freedom. The question, as always, is: what do you want?

1 What have you been taught or what do you believe regarding authority? Take some time to reflect and write about it.

2 Often Christians use the word "authority" when talking about things in the spiritual realm. What does that mean to you? What sorts of emotions does this bring up in you?

Take a few breaths and feel your insides a bit. In the space below, spend some time drawing your ideas of what authority "looks" like. You can draw an action scene if you want. Feel free to put yourself or others into the art.

Love is what we were born with.
Fear is what we learned here.
- *Marianne Williamson*

We can easily forgive a child who is afraid of the dark; the real tragedy of life is when men are afraid of the light.
- *Plato*

My friend Pete talks about how we, in our unconsciousness, are a lot like zombies: we just keep slowly moving towards our destruction with no idea we're doing it, our only thought to keep consuming whatever it is we think will sustain us. Like I said before, we end up eating ourselves. And our fears, pain, and addictions are fine with that. They love the idea that we're afraid of them and that we deny their existence and that none of the people who claim a belief in the power of God have ever manifested any of that power. They just keep creating suffering and feeding on it.

Guided Meditation

Let's finish with a guided meditation that will be a combination of two of the exercises in this chapter: the body check-in and the drawing. Begin with closing your eyes and breathing deeply and slowly, feeling your body. By now, if you have been practicing this, you are probably becoming pretty sensitive to what you feel inside, even if that feeling is numbness. Wait until you are centered and then use your imagination to recall the picture you drew to represent your ideas on authority. See the drawings coming together and, when they are complete, take some time to look at them in your mind. Make note of what you experience in your body. If you begin to feel things stir in response to the pictures, speak to the feelings and to the pictures. Helpful phrases are prayers of authority like, "Show yourself," or questions like, "What are you?"

Your experience may be physical or it may not. Either way, use this exercise to gain more sensitivity to what is happening deep down. If you are shining a light inward, the beings that dwell in the shadows won't stay there for long; the darkness simply can't comprehend the light. If you do experience a manifestation, just know your pain only has the power you give it. If you feel fear, it isn't because you have something to fear, but only because you perceive you have something to fear.

These types of confrontations are how we begin to learn what authority is. You may feel the need to go to war—but this is not necessary. If you feel like fighting, that is understandable and completely okay—I've wielded a sword in my spirit many times - just make note of why you needed to go there. And the next time you experience something like this, see if you can stand more in your authority and less in a strength based in violence. God is with you—and this is all the power you need.

In the following pages, write about your experience of this meditation.

❧ Selah ❧

CHAPTER 7

Consciousness

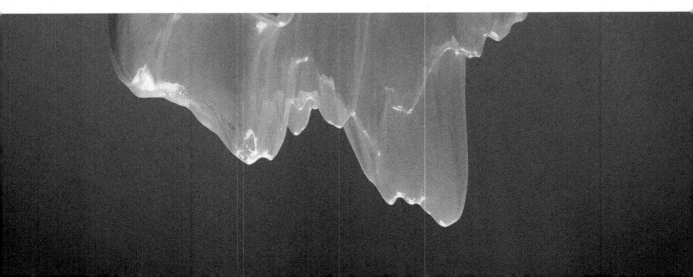

There is no coming to consciousness without pain. People will do anything, no matter how absurd, in order to avoid facing their own Soul.

One does not become enlightened by imagining figures of light, but by making the darkness conscious.

- *Carl Jung*

Seeing under the surface is seeing more.

In this chapter, we are going to discuss the idea of consciousness. I recognize that this word has been sort of filed away into the folder marked "new age" for so many people, especially Christians, but we are going to attempt to redeem its use because it is an extremely helpful word in dealing with addiction. The truth is, most of this guidebook has been about consciousness, but hopefully this chapter will tie it all together a bit. If you have been practicing the things in this guidebook, you have most likely increased your consciousness, so this may make complete sense. If you haven't practiced the techniques I have been talking about, this may be more difficult, but just know that consciousness is THE goal. And you must do something to get there.

If you are an addict, then somewhere in your unconscious, you believe your addictive behavior is the best thing for you. A part of you believes this because the truth of what you are medicating with that addiction is too painful to face. That truth, if brought into the light, can rob you of the things you perceive are holding you together, like your beliefs or your language. You may come to this consciousness as well and then deal with some of the loss of certainty that accompanies that.

But there is an upside to this, because as Richard Rohr says,

> "People who've had any genuine spiritual experience always know that they don't know. They are utterly humbled before mystery. They are in awe before the abyss of it all, in wonder at eternity and depth, and a Love which is incomprehensible to the mind."

And I would add that these people are at peace with it all. When things are brought into the light, The Kingdom of God that Jesus said was around us and in us becomes visible. And one discovers God has been there all along—this is what the Jewish people call shalom. All things are as God intended.

So, in this chapter, we will continue the work of gaining consciousness. We will begin once again with a body check-in and then move into some contemplation regarding our thought processes.

BODY CHECK IN

Like always, take three deep, slow breaths and sit completely still. Lay down if that feels more comfortable. The goal here is to feel what is in your body without thinking and judging—just observing. What do you feel? Try to circle the part of your body where you feel something and then write about it in the spaces provided below.

Try to describe the feelings in your body in as much detail as you can (and remember that feeling "nothing" is a definitive feeling—if you are numb, it is important to note that.)

Consciousness is a way of seeing—this has been what these body check-ins have been about. We are trying to gain a new consciousness of what is in us and around us.

This chapter's exercises will be a series of three guided meditations. Make sure you read through the entire instruction for each one and understand it before you begin. It is also helpful to pray before you begin—ask God for the presence and strength to move into these things, because if you do, it will undoubtedly be painful.

The Spirit of God is ready and willing to open our eyes and help us see God, creation, and ourselves in a whole new light. If you have been doing the meditations in this book all along, this will not be difficult. If you haven't, you may find it challenging. Either way, the key for these is that you do them. Don't just read about them and then think about them—this will do nothing more than assign this process to the category of "intellect," which will produce nothing more than various beliefs, but little actual change.

Meditation #1 *The Explorer*

Creation is amazing. Even if you live in a place where nothing grows, there is always something to notice. But can we stop and be still enough to notice that all around us all the time are pieces of our Creator—things that carry the breath of life in them?

Annie Dillard says, "The answer must be, I think, that beauty and grace are performed whether or not we will or sense them. The least we can do is try to be there." So, in this meditation, we are just going to try to take some time to notice. I practice this by taking walks with my young daughter without having an agenda. I go at her pace and try to notice whatever she notices. This was difficult for me at first, but I have learned how to be present with her over time.

You can do this alone or with your dog or with a friend, but stopping and noticing is the key. And when you stop, determine whether your body feels uncomfortable or not. Is there a part of you that is trying to get going? Is it difficult to truly observe a tree, an ant, a flower, or a creek? Can you be still? If not, why not? Don't judge yourself—there is no right or wrong way to do this. There is only observation. Can you be with yourself well?

It might be helpful to leave your watch inside and there is no question that your phone will be a problem. Just set it down and forget it exists for a few minutes. And remember; this isn't about quantity, it's about quality. If you can be truly present for 10 minutes, it is better than an hour of your mind racing and your agenda waiting for you back home.

When you get done, spend some time writing about the experience. Don't just write about what you saw—the more important stuff is what you experienced internally as you learned to notice. You have the following pages to make notes on that...

Meditation #2 *The Listener*

This meditation will be a little more of a challenge emotionally. In fact, it might be very difficult, so let me explain what it is before I explain how to do it. You're going to think of three people who either know you well or with whom you have interacted a great deal in your life. Exclude only your parents. People you barely know or whom you only know in a shallow way will have little value for this meditation. Write their names here:

1)   2)   3)

Listed at the bottom of this page are three questions. The goal is to go to each person with a request for an honest conversation. Explain to them that you are doing some work on yourself and that you want to hear some honest opinions from them about you. If a person is unwilling, just move on. If they are willing, bring this book with you, ask the three questions and jot notes in it afterward. The notes should be about:

1) What they said and

2) How that made you feel.

This is a therapeutic technique that could be called a type of "relational therapy," based on the belief that people often can see the real us in ways we cannot. The question is: Do we have the humility to hear them and then observe what we feel inside?

As they talk, you may feel anger arise and defensiveness take over. This exercise will require you to observe those emotions internally and not judge them, while still allowing yourself to feel them. Ask yourself this basic question:

If what they are saying is true, what does that mean for me?

The 3 Questions:

1) Please tell me what you honestly feel are my two greatest strengths (first) and then my two greatest weaknesses (last).

2) What is your experience of me when we talk? Do you feel heard and seen? Do you feel like I am open or vulnerable?

3) Is there anything you wish I would be willing to hear, but you feel I am not?

No problem can be solved from the same level of consciousness that created it.

- Albert Einstein

Meditation #3 *The Watcher*

This meditation will require you to find a place of silence and stillness. What I want you to try is at least 15 minutes of deep breathing. If this is easy for you, make it longer. But there is a very specific guided imagery I want you to employ in this meditation: you'll once more become "The Watcher."

Lie down or sit comfortably and begin your breathing. Feel your body internally and try to keep your mind from racing. If it does, don't judge it; simply observe it. Sometimes it helps to cover your eyes with a blindfold of some sort. When you are ready, begin the following scenario in your mind:

You are beginning your addictive ritual. Everyone who is an addict has one. We separate from ourselves a bit and then begin the routine that leads to the payoff. But instead of seeing yourself as the person engaging in the ritual, stand back some distance. Simply watch. Sit across the room or follow your other self wherever they go. Don't judge them. You know how they feel and the situation calls for compassion, not conviction—love, not condemnation.

When you are ready, before too long into the process, walk up to the other you and engage them. Look them in the eye. Say something to them. (Ex: "You don't have to do this.") The Watcher in you is your spirit; it has the wisdom needed to speak life into this other part of you. Observe how the other "you" reacts. Engage the relationship.

What you are doing in this meditation is simply engaging consciously the parts of you that are always at work but that you are usually not conscious of. As we said before, addiction is unconscious suffering—but we know that it is only a part of you that is dependent on sex or porn or substances to survive the pain you carry. The other part of you is alive and has the power to sustain you and heal you. That is your spirit and it is the part of us that is one with God.

In the following pages, write about your experience with this meditation. Feel free to repeat it as much as you desire and with any scenario you desire. Your spirit is real and it is ready and waiting to be used. And God is with you.

∾ Selah ∾

CHAPTER 8

Sexuality as Connection

Love is not something we give or get;
it is something that we nurture and
grow, a connection that can only be
cultivated between two people when
it exists within each one of them —
we can only love others as much as
we love ourselves.

- *Brene Brown*

Our sexuality is a deep spiritual expression.

It is meant to magnetize us and allow us to experience the essence of the world. In the act of sexual intimacy with another, we find one of the deepest of these expressions. It is where we find acceptance and value and true vulnerability. If we allow our hearts to be open in this way, this connection can take us past the mere enjoyment of our world and into the mystery of each other. This mystery mirrors the mystery we find in God.

Sexuality is a gateway for spirit. And just as God inhabits the essence of all of life, God is in our sexuality. This is why it is so significant that the creation poem in the book of Genesis describes humanity being created "naked and without shame." Seen through this lens, the part of us that connected us to God, creation, each other, and our world was completely whole and functioning perfectly. I believe this passage in the Bible is referring to sexuality. When "the fall" took place and Adam and Eve hid from God, the text says they sewed fig leaves together to cover themselves. They had become ashamed of themselves. A wound in their sexuality had entered into their consciousness and as a result, they were disconnected from all things, including each other. God even asks them, "Who told you that you were naked?"

They were completely unaware of the breach that had taken place. Their state of consciousness had changed. And their sexuality became something that functioned like a computer with a virus. Chaos ensued in humanity's connection to everything. This is why we find our greatest corruption within that connection.

So when I talk about healing our sexuality and bringing it into alignment with what God intended for us, it isn't about trying to decode what God intended for us and trying harder and harder to do whatever those things are. It's about going to the place inside us where this connection was broken and healing those wounds. Then the way will be made clear and we will be able to hear the Spirit speaking to us. We will be able to hear the voice of the Creator declaring his creation, including us, good. In that state, shame is lifted and we can know peace.

So, in this chapter, we are going to write about sexuality more than sex. But we are also going to do some meditation that is designed to go into our sexuality and hear the whisper of God to our spirits.

Let's begin in the body.

BODY CHECK IN

Like always, take three deep, slow breaths and sit completely still. Lay down if that feels more comfortable. The goal here is to feel what is in your body without thinking and judging—just observing. What do you feel in your body? Try to circle the part of your body where you feel something and then write about it in the spaces provided below.

Try to describe the feelings in your body in as much detail as you can (and remember that feeling "nothing" is a definitive feeling—if you are numb, it is important to note that.

Sexuality is ultimately what connects us to ourselves. It is an experience in your spirit. This experience of feeling your body that we have been working on is an experience of your sexuality. As you have been learning how to feel, you've been using your sexuality to do so.

Intimacy is not a happy medium. It is a way of being in which the tension between distance and closeness is dissolved and a new horizon appears. Intimacy is beyond fear.

- Henri Nouwen

Exercise *A guided meditation*

Below are four sentences. Pick a sentence and, when you're ready, sit down on the floor, take three deep breaths, close your eyes, and say your chosen sentence as you exhale. Say it three times slowly and intentionally. Observe how it makes you feel. Understand that by saying these things, you are doing nothing wrong, but if you feel guilt, shame, pain, or numbness anywhere (meaning that those feelings will manifest in your body—perhaps a knot in the stomach or tightness in the chest or an inability to feel anything at all), then make a note of it.

Some of these statements might not be "true" as you understand it consciously, but try to say them anyway, because some of them may trigger emotions inside you that are important to pay attention to. Don't get hung up on whether you believe the sentence to be morally okay. You are two people, both conscious and unconscious, and this work is meant to create a greater connection between the two by the awakening and empowering of your spirit.

Here are the sentences:

1) My name is _____ and I am a sexual person.

2) My body has been given to me and I can do whatever I want with it without shame.

3) I find _____ to be erotic and sexy and that's okay.

4) This is my body. Every part of it is beautiful and sexy.

Now sit with those feelings and simply breathe for a while. Try not to let your mind race and cut you off from what you are feeling inside.

Did the sentences make you uncomfortable? How do you feel? Right now, you might feel nothing. You might feel anger. You might be ready to explode in tears.

Whatever it is, keep your awareness there. Just feel those feelings without judgment. When you are ready, spend some time journaling your experience of the exercise.

Finally, take some time to journal about what you truly want to change about your sexuality. As you write, observe whether the changes you want to make are rooted in shame or in something different.

Can you hold the desire to not be an addict and at the same time understand that your desires are not "wrong", but merely unconscious? Addiction is a person stumbling in the darkness, and the Spirit is the light that draws you out.

❧ Selah ❧

CHAPTER 9
Processing

Until you make the unconscious conscious, it will direct your life and you will call it fate.

- Carl Jung

If it were easy, everyone would do it.

Throughout this guidebook, we have been meditating—learning to listen to our bodies, to our spirits, and ultimately, to God. In this chapter, I want to discuss a nuance to the art of meditation. It's called processing. This is simply using meditation to heal pain and move it out of our bodies. I find it helpful to refer to the pain as energy.

I am aware of the new-age connotations here, but the word "energy" is helpful because it is way of summing up the variety of things we are moving out of our bodies. Throughout this book, we've been talking about all the different things that get lodged within us and keep us unconscious: emotional wounds, other people's pain, etc. It's all accounted for with the word "energy." Energy is something you can feel—and the key to all of this from the beginning was feeling.

Processing is simply allowing what is in us to come out. In other words, when we practice feeling what is in our bodies, like we have in each of these chapters, we then learn to allow our spirits to expel that energy. This can take on all kinds of forms. You might have already started to process as you've been practicing. For instance, when you feel your body, it may have made you want to do things like cough or even throw up. You might have felt the urge to scream or rage. These are all attempts your body is making at moving out some of the toxic energy trapped inside you.

So, in this chapter, we will use a six-step process. Make sure you read the entirety of the teaching before you begin. If you have been practicing the meditations, you will have already started to learn these things at a certain level and they will feel somewhat familiar. Some of you may have even started to learn your own way of processing and know there is truth in it because you can feel it changing you. The Spirit works that way—speaking to each of us in a way that we understand or need. If this is the case, don't let me rob you of your experience. You have the Spirit of God inside of you, and That can be trusted to lead you.

The steps I will describe are a basic way of understanding this. They are simple and easy to understand. The complexity comes in the application of them. Doing is always more complicated than understanding, simply because our pain is invested in staying put and will put up resistance.

This time, treat the Body check-in as the "warm-up" for the process.

BODY CHECK IN

Take three deep, slow breaths and sit completely still. Lay down if that feels more comfortable. The goal here is to feel what is in your body without thinking and judging—just observing. What do you feel in your body? Try to circle the part of your body where you feel something and then write about it in the spaces provided below.

Try to describe the feelings in your body in as much detail as you can and remember that feeling "nothing" is a definitive feeling—if you are numb, it is important to note that.

Even numbness can be moved out of the body. It's a very distinctive energy, so be prepared to feel it.

10 Minutes of Silence

A Guided Process from Feel Like Redemption: The Pilgrimage to Health and Healing

This exercise is both very simple and very difficult at the same time:

1) Find somewhere quiet and dark where you can sit or lay down.

You need quiet and darkness because the mind tends to grab onto any stimulus very quickly and start heading some odd direction. It drives us from our bodies into our heads instantly. It is the ever-present noise of our culture. Yes, I am saying technology does damage in this way. If you can't get somewhere dark, cover your eyes with a blindfold of some sort, but silence is essential. Sometimes ambient sounds can help, but be careful to observe if your mind races somewhere else because of the sounds or if the sounds help you feel your internal self. When I first heard my brother's stories about his processes and tried to implement what he did, I used our bedroom closet, which was just big enough for me to lie down. At times, when trying to access my pain, my body would shut down and put me to sleep. If that happens to you, simply observe it without judgment. You probably need the rest anyway.

2) Begin by breathing slowly. Fill your entire body with air.

The Bible, in its original languages, speaks of the ruach (in Hebrew) or the pneuma (in Greek) of God, which are words that mean both "breath" and "spirit" or "soul" of God. For instance, in the creation story in Genesis, when God created man, the text says God breathed the "breath of life" into man. "The Spirit of Life" is another way to understand this. For this reason, many cultures have understood that breathing is an important part of spiritual meditation and the experience of God.

Again, this isn't as easy as it sounds. Hopefully through the process of this guidebook, you have been practicing breathing. If so, this will be easier for you than those who have not. As you begin to breathe, focus your attention on your breath. You will notice that your mind will try to jump in and start the race again. When I first was on the floor in the closet, I could only get five or six breaths out before my mind would start racing and then my breathing would get harder. As my body would relax, sometimes my chest would get heavy. This, as I understand it now, was the process of my body going into shutdown/protective mode. The breath has a way of opening up the body to feel what's inside, and if your body has been trained to keep pain and emotion suppressed, the defenses may come up very fast and try to shut down the breath. It's okay, though. Just keep breathing—faster if you need to. This is where using some guided imagery in your mind can be helpful to focus the mind and allow some room for the body to step in and feel. We have done some of that in this guidebook, but in brief, it simply means that you imagine a narrative in your mind, perhaps recalling a time where you were triggered, or imagining an interaction with the object or person that triggers your pain. Even imagining yourself hiking or running up a mountain can help create focus.

3) Feel, don't think.

For ten minutes, give your mind a vacation from running your world. Your goal here is to breathe for ten minutes and feel what's in your body. Hopefully this has become easier over the course of this guidebook. Remember, we're not attempting to transform your whole universe or teleport you to Heaven and back. The goal is to go inward and simply feel. Observe what happens as you do this. Again, notice if your mind starts racing. Don't judge it as good or bad—that's simply unhelpful. If your mind begins racing, try to silence it again. If it helps, locate the pain like we have been doing with the body check-ins. It's especially helpful to feel the places where you most carry your stress. For instance, many people, myself included, experience a tremendous amount of their stress in their stomachs or in their chests. When my friend Pat gets triggered, he feels something painful in his middle-lower back. If you are able to feel these sensations (or any sensation including numbness which feels like the absence of feeling all together), you are already experiencing a deeper awareness of yourself.

I often ask people, "What are you feeling?" and their answer is something like "I'm feeling angry" or "I'm frustrated." Those are what we can call secondary emotions—they are the emotion over the top of the deeper emotion. This is very important because we could very easily stop with these emotions and attempt to control them, but they are generated from a wound underneath. For instance, anger may be how the true pain manifests, because most of us carry wounds that warrant real anger. But what is the actual reason we are angry? That is the true emotion underneath. In my case, I have discovered a great deal of pain from the experience of emotional abandonment within myself. Of course anger is generated from that experience, and for good reason. I have carried most of it from a very young age. The anger might need to be moved or even experienced in order to be healed, but to do that in meditation, we seek to feel the actual pain in our bodies.

4) Pray—because God is with you.

Remember that prayer is the act of talking to God, while meditation is the act of listening to God. Know this: God is with you. But in this step, I am not saying to take over the conversation. I am saying that as you do this process, it is possible you will begin to feel things in your body. You might feel something you are familiar with but perhaps had never focused on before. A prayer that can be helpful here is something very simple such as: place your hand over the area in your body that you are feeling the pain/discomfort/familiar weirdness and say something like, "Show me what this is." That simple. There are very few words required in our prayer when our intent is on allowing the Spirit to move inside of us. But, for reasons I can't say I fully understand, I believe speaking things aloud is important. Perhaps it's because one of the things that becomes suppressed inside of us is our voice. We struggle to speak the truth we feel and must therefore learn to speak again, just like we have to learn to feel again. God is with you, whether you know it or not and your prayer is heard and understood.

Continued...

5) Find Your Emotional Truth

When I first began this process of allowing the Spirit to heal me and awaken my dormant spirit inside of my body, I discovered that there was some "truth" inside of me that was tough to categorize. My brother uses the term "emotional truth" in FLR. I think that is helpful. We're not talking about fact. We're talking about the truth of the emotional experience.

As we pray in this process, there in the closet or on your bed or in your car or wherever you are, we must be able to be honest emotionally about what we're experiencing. Know that God is not afraid of your pain or doubt or anger. Jesus understood this deeply and screamed it out from his core. In fact, throughout the Hebrew Scriptures, we see a tradition of people blasting God with their agony and experience. This cannot be ignored. God sees us. So keep breathing and be honest. God hears you. So feel that pain and observe it. And withhold judgment of yourself.

6) Be prepared to let some things out.

As you've been learning to breathe, feel, and pray truthfully, your spirit has been activated. This process is one of asking your spirit and the Spirit of God to heal you. You might have struggled to feel anything at first, but if you keep working in this way, it's simply a matter of time until it begins.

If you feel nothing or numbness, that is still feeling *something*. Underneath the "nothing" is a thing you have always felt but have repressed. You have been medicating that thing for so long and once you do feel it, your spirit is going to start to try to kick it out of your body. For me, it started with coughing. You might have been experiencing this reaction or something like it already. In my story, I carried butterflies in my stomach for five years without ceasing. When I started processing, the more intensely I would feel those butterflies, the more I would cough. Sometimes I would yawn. I even threw up. Sometimes, I would want to scream because the rage was so intense that I grabbed a pillow, put my face into it, and let it out. I even did this in the mountains when no one was around. And I spent a great deal of time weeping because so much of the pain that was trapped inside of my body was really a mountain of grief.

I found that afterward, I often felt very different, like some part of me had moved out and been replaced with something far better. Sometimes I would feel peace. Sometimes I would feel like I had just disturbed a hornets' nest and there was a great deal more work to do. At first that part scared me, but I learned, as you will, to stand in my authority and move them out of me as well.

If this is what you experience, it is very important to continue working, though perhaps not that day. Your pain will continue to resist being removed. Don't stop—dare yourself to move time and time again. No matter what I experienced, every time I would do this, I would learn something. A great deal of this learning revolved around my ability to hear the voice of the Spirit of God and decide that, as He led me into the unknown, I could trust that voice. This is the place where all of my belief became something that placed boots on the road. This is where my pilgrimage grew legs and began to walk.

The Process in Brief

So, to review the basics of processing:

1) Find somewhere quiet and dark where you can sit or lay down.

2) Begin by breathing slowly. Fill your entire body with air.

3) Feel, don't think.

4) Pray—because God is with you.

5) Find your emotional truth.

6) Be prepared to let some things out.

You can take as much time as you want, but I would say that your minimum goal should
be ten minutes of processing to begin with. If you have been practicing, this should be achievable. If not, it is a good place to start. You can certainly do it for less time, but in my
experience, it takes at least five minutes or so before you start to feel the resistance that comes along with actual spiritual practice. If you can come to that place and stay engaged there for another five minutes, you will begin to experience things that propel you down
the path of healing.

These experiences can look very different for everyone, but they will move you forward. As you move forward, you can take more time, gaining wisdom as you start to have experiences that change you. The importance is doing this on a regular basis, daily if you can. Ten minutes should be doable daily for just about everyone and as you do this, you can begin to couple it with other types of therapy that present themselves to you as helpful. But you will always be moving forward.

A human being has so many skins inside, covering the depths of the heart. We know so many things, but we don't know ourselves! Why, thirty or forty skins or hides, as thick and hard as an ox's or bear's, cover the soul. Go into your own ground and learn to know yourself there.

- *Meister Eckhart*

Processing is about peeling back the layers of pain you carry and healing them.

Like I said before, it's where the idea of freedom grows legs and starts to walk. Below is some space to journal about your experiences or to write down your thoughts on processing. If you have questions and details you wish to be able to recall, make sure you write them down.

Each time you process, you will have unique experiences — make sure you take note of them. Use this space for reflection, but remember that reflection and contemplation can only get you so far. You must develop your spiritual practice. This is what will awaken your spirit and lead you into freedom. God is with you and my prayer for you is that you gain the courage to act.

For the gift of this new day

for waking again from the dreams of the night

for our bodies strengthened and our minds renewed

thanks be to you, O God.

You are the stillness of the night

You are the genesis of the morning

You are the moistness of new conception.

Let there be peace in the human soul

let there be wakings to new consciousness

let there be tears of love.

In the life of the world this day

and in our own hearts

let there be fresh tears of love.

John Philip Newell, *Praying With the Earth*

❧ Selah ❧

The Road

The future was uncertain, absolutely, and there were many hurdles, twists, and turns to come, but as long as I kept moving forward, one foot in front of the other, the voices of fear and shame, the messages from those who wanted me to believe that I wasn't good enough, would be stilled.

- *Chris Gardner, The Pursuit of Happyness*

Are not two sparrows sold for a cent? And yet not one of them will fall to the ground apart from your Father. But the very hairs of your head are all numbered. So do not fear; you are more valuable than many sparrows.

- *Jesus Christ—Matthew, chapter 10, verses 29-31*

In 2013, I went on my first actual traditional Christian pilgrimage. I was starting a new chapter in my life, having quit my sales career in pursuit of a life as a writer and teacher. My wife told me that it was important that I mark that time in my life as sacred—that I have a memory I would never forget and could always return to, a memory that would speak to me of the journey I had been on and to the loving presence of the One who had walked with me on the road. My graduate school was offering a weeklong pilgrimage to the holy island of Iona in northern Scotland as a for-credit "spiritual formation" class. The pilgrimage was meant to be an experience of deep contemplation, memory-making, community, meditation, and exploration of the ancient Celtic Christian tradition, both theologically and in practice.

It was on Iona, while walking alone one day along a rock wall made by my ancestors close to 3,000 years ago, that I came to fully realize that I had been living most of my life in a world where all things were black and white and that as human beings, we simply weren't made in that mold. In the world I understood, there were only winners and losers; right and wrong; true and false; good and evil. I realized in that moment that being human was not compatible with this type of thinking and neither was God. I still see people say things all the time like, "Sin is sin" and talk about how a holy God cannot handle the presence of sin. We take transcendent things like love, grace, forgiveness, and hope and try to turn them into concrete structures with instruction manuals and rulebooks. We try to force square pegs into round holes. And what has resulted is the crisis of addiction and depression and anxiety we have before us.

As I thought about these things, I remember looking at that wall and wondering how my bloodline journeyed from building that wall all that time ago on an island in Scotland to the writing of the book you are currently reading—a work of passion and caffeine consumption in the coffee shops of Seattle. I marveled at the length and complexity of that road. And then I realized that being a human created in the image of God wasn't about reading the Bible and trying to become like God. It was about trying to become fully human. And that isn't a war or a set of rules. It's a road that we walk. It's a trail into the unknown. And it cannot be done without the experience of our spirits being made alive. We must be born again. And by that, I don't mean converted to Christianity, though I gratefully find myself under the broad wings of that tradition. I mean we must walk into the *new* in ways that crucify our identities, so we can be resurrected. The types of practices detailed in this guidebook are helping me accomplish this; I believe they can help you, too.

St. Iraneus said that "The Glory of God is Man fully alive." For those of us who are walking this sacred journey through addiction and into freedom, we must take that quote and understand that to walk is to live. God is not waiting in His glory for you to arrive. He is walking the road with you and in you, glorying in the journey in the here and now.

So, here in the conclusion of this guidebook, I am going to ask you to reflect some on the road both behind you and ahead of you. I will have some reflective questions for you to help with some of the thought; but, first let's do another body-check in. My hope is that you have gained the ability over the course of this guidebook to truly meditate and feel your body internally.

BODY CHECK IN

Like always, take three deep, slow breaths and sit completely still. Lay down if that feels more comfortable. The goal here is to feel what is in your body without thinking and judging—just observing. What do you feel in your body? Try to circle the part of your body where you feel something and then write about it in the spaces provided below.

Try to describe the feelings in your body in as much detail as you can (and remember that feeling "nothing" is a definitive feeling—if you are numb, it is important to note that.)

This might be easy for you by now. Remember that there is no right or wrong here—the experience is just feeling. If you can process right here, go for it. Remember that processing is simply letting things out of your body.

Man is a creature who walks in two worlds and traces upon the walls of his cave the wonders and the nightmare experiences of his spiritual pilgrimage.

- *Morris West*

Thinking back to where you were at the beginning of this process, what's changed the most? Have you changed in ways you expected or were you surprised?

Religion points to that area of human experience where in one way or another man comes upon mystery as a summons to pilgrimage.

- Frederick Buechner

What, if anything, has changed about your beliefs? What role do you see your beliefs playing in your transformation?

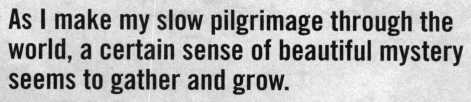

As I make my slow pilgrimage through the world, a certain sense of beautiful mystery seems to gather and grow.

- A.C. Benson

Let's talk about what we don't know. What things, if any, do you feel are a mystery to you? What are your deepest and most honest questions you have? What doubts do you carry with you on this leg of the journey and into the next?

Faith is not the clinging to a shrine but an endless pilgrimage of the heart.

- *Abraham Joshua Heschel*

In this final page, I could try to write something beautiful and inspirational. I could write a prayer or put some more awesome quotes about how this transformational journey of life through God's complex creation is a crazy, difficult, painful, stunning, awe-inspiring, breathtaking, powerful experience. But the truth is, I need to leave. I have my pilgrimage to walk and must leave you to yours. So, in this last page, take some time to breathe and to contemplate the road ahead and what your prayer is for that road.

Remember, prayer is an intention. You don't have to beg—The Kingdom of God is within you and Jesus said that if we seek after that, all things would be given to us.

My prayers go forward to all who choose this road. I leave it to you to finish this book….

❧ Selah ❧

Extra Journal Space....